With Our Baggage

With Our Baggage

Alan Berecka

LAMAR UNIVERSITY press

ISBN: 978-0-9852552-9-9
Library of Congress Control Number: 2013944473

Cover Design: Gerardo Cobarruvias
Manufactured in the United States

Lamar University Press
Beaumont, Texas

Dedicated to the memory of my parents
Stella (Puch) and Albert Berecka

Other books of Poetry from Lamar University Press:
David Bowles, *Flower, Song, Dance,* Aztec *and Mayan*
Poetry (a new translation)
Jeffrey DeLotto, *Voices Writ in Sand*
Mimi Ferebee, *Wildfires and Atmospheric Memories*
Michelle Hartman, *Disenchanted and Disgruntled*
Dave Oliphant, *The Pilgrimage, Selected Poems: 1962-2012*
Carol Coffee Reposa, *Underground Musicians*

For information on these and other Lamar University Press books go to
www.LamarUniversityPress.Org

Acknowledgments

I am grateful to all those who aided in the production of this book. To Sara Kaplan and Angela O'Donnell for agreeing to be first readers of the manuscript and their suggestions which improved the final draft. To Ruth Dunn and Alice Berecka for helping to proof the manuscript, Jerry Cobar-ruvias for helping with the cover and head shot, and to Jerry Craven for publishing the finished product.

I'd like to thank all of those who helped me with my baggage along the way, especially Pete Merkl for deciding we should yell something in Polish at John Paul II in Rome back in 1979, to Paul Boer and Mike Guadagnoli for helping me finish all those pitchers of beer, for Janis Graves for riding along in the back seat of our parents' car for all those years, for Rachael and Aaron for turning out well despite my baggage and to Alice my Sky Chief in Chief who has put up with way too much of said baggage.

I appreciate the editors of the following journals and anthologies for publishing some of the poems in this book.

Beacons

The Blue Rock Review

The Christian Century

The Comic Flaw

The Concho River Review

CyberSoliel

Druskininkai Poetic Fall 2010

Each Man has One Life

El Grito del Lobo Slimsides

Elegant Rage: A Poetic Tribute to
    Woody Guthrie

The Enigmatist

Forget Guttenberg Broadsides

Leveling the Field

St. Peter's B-list: Contemporary
    Poems Inspired by the Saints

MO: Writings from the River

Octopus Beak Inc

Penwood Review

Red River Review

Remembering the Body

Right Hand Pointing

The San Antonio Express

Slow Trains

Two Southwests

Windhover

Contents

Part I

1   What I Now Know
2   Grubbing
3   Born Again: Polish in South Texas
4   Why I am Not a Nature Poet
5   The Preserver
6   Provenance
7   A Parrot Head's Wasted Thoughts
8   Hand Set Lust
9   The Heraclitean Urn
10   Reviewing *Booklist*
11   Lesson on *Poetics*
12   Reading Answers
13   The Burden of Genius
14   Columbo and the Three Bears
16   Happy Ending
17   The Way it Is
18   Taxed
19   An Old Man Looks at Leadership
20   After the Roll
21   Clint Hartung Remembers
22   Solitude
23   Prisoners
24   Oblivion
26   Show Business
27   The Oracle's Art
28   One Man's Garbage
29   Library Patrons and Conservation
30   The Naked Truth
31   God's Radio
32   Skeletons
34   Nearly Gay Pride
35   Keys to Insanity
36   The American Nest
37   Art Appreciation
38   The Limits of Art
39   Old School
40   Bliss
41   And So it Goes
42   My Life Among the Birds
44   Crapping Out
45   Act V
46   Leveling
47   Good Friday
48   Battle Cry
50   Signs and Sacraments

Part II

55   Awash
57   By Any Name
58   Finding the Spirit
59   Belle de Jour
60   St. Peter's Square 1979
61   Sniping
62   Reflection
63   Lost in Translation
65   Temperance
66   Child Rearing
68   Reconciliation
71   A Father's Confession
73   Thinking Out of the Box
74   Resonance
75   Throwing Hail Marys
77   The Fruit
79   A Better Way
80   For My Daughter as She Leaves Home
81   Remembering the Body
82   Momma Tried
83   Holy War
84   Excused Absence
85   The Downside of Transubstantiation
86   The Upside of Transubstantiation
87   Why Not Consubstantiation
88   The Island Revisited
89   The Sacrament of Marriage
90   More Than Bread
91   Silver Anniversary Flight
92   Winter Wedding
93   The Body
95   Meditation on the Orthodox Liturgical Prayer
96   Easter Vigil
98   Commuting
99   Meaning

Part I

What I Now Know

What did I know, what did I know...
—*Those Winter Sundays*, Robert Hayden

We sat for a moment on the metal bench
just this side of security. Her final Christmas
break over, my daughter held on to her photo i.d.
and boarding pass with a diamond adorned hand.

We made small talk when the notion
swept over me like a black wave—she
would not return to be home ever again.
All my past disappointments revisited me.
They poked at bruises and scars as we stood
to hug. The embrace returned me to the side
of my mother's cancer ward bed. My spring
break over, I stood to return to my school life,
my wife and our infant daughter. My mother
reached up and draped her arms around my neck.
She pulled me down toward her with more strength
than I thought she had left. I echoed her affection
and returned her kiss.

                  I regained my balance
in time to watch my daughter merge
into the line of departing passengers.

Grubbing

As kids we used to ask each other,
So what are you? I always answered,
I'm Lithuanian. Never mind
my mother was Polish, never
mind a half-century had passed since
my father's folks had disembarked.
So now after my trip to Vilnius
my friends ask if I found my roots.

I found the same aroma that filled
my Grandma's house—onions frying
in butter—in most of the restaurants.
I found my Grandpa's insistence
that he be joined in his next stiff drink
in all the bars. I heard the same spoken
cadence filled with its rolled r's, zoos,
chews and hard consonants that once bounced
off my grandparents' tongues fly by
still a foot over my head. I found hints
of their long-gone faces—their complexion
and Baltic bone structure—in the sternness
of strangers who never made eye contact
as they bustled by me on the crowded sidewalks
and cobblestone streets.

                But mostly I found
that I am no Alex Haley. I am just a man
with a short history who once plunked
down five litas to buy a Big Mac.

Born Again: Polish in South Texas

Judging from Juan's face, I shouldn't have said,
Funny, ain't it? Whenever the diversity committee
brings someone in, they're always Hispanic.

Juan puts down his menu and starts to talk
about the lack of Mexican media role models
and then says, *You Anglos just don't understand.*

And I think to myself, *Anglo?* As if
I was not raised on kapusta, kielbasa,
pierogi, and gwumpki, as if

my grandparents had not spoken broken
English at their mill jobs and their
native tongue while at home, as if

as a kid, I did not have to listen to Louey
B. Zigienkowski spin Little Wally polkas
every Sunday on the ride to mass, as if

the last smart Polack on TV was not
Banacek, played by George Peppard
who really was Anglo, as if ever since

I moved south of the Brazos my history
has been erased—white washed
into that of some tea-swilling, scones-
eating, Queen-loving Englishman.

But Juan is a good friend, and since
we are all guilty of painting the other
with broad strokes, I nod and say,

Maybe so. I reach across the table
and dunk a corn chip into our salsa.
We sit quietly, reading our menus,
considering our next course.

3

Why I am Not a Nature Poet

My old man grew up tough
and poor a block from the mills
in Utica. I grew up out in the sticks
between cow pastures, intrigued
by my friends who wore blue uniforms
with yellow bandanas to school.

One night at supper I asked
my dad if I could join
the Cub Scouts. Confused
and a little pissed, he put
down his beer and said,
*What the hell do you want
to do that for; you got
a backyard, don't you?*

The Preserver

My office phone rings; some student says
his English teacher gave him my name,
told him I was a real writer. I'm wondering
what new ex-friend ratted me out. The kid
rambles on, says he needs help; he can't stop
writing. He says, *Words keep flowing like blood
from a deep gash*; this craziness is ruining
his life, consuming him whole; he's at 500
pages and running. *Jesus*, I think, *he wants
me to read this thing,* but he just keeps talking,
tells me he's not the literary type, reads
the box scores in the paper, that's all,
but now this. He's so scared, he saw
a shrink who asked him about his mother
and gave him pills that put him to sleep.

I ask him what genre he's working in.
I figure if it's prose, I can weasel out.
He says he has no idea what I'm talking
about. I say, *You know is it a story
or a poem.* He says, *It's not like that;
it's more like a universe.* He asks
what he should do. I'm stumped,
but I tell him, *Keep writing; this must
be happening for a reason.* He thanks me,
but I can sense his desperation as the line
goes dead. I wonder if I did the right thing,
but I think there is a chance that in some new
and slightly askew universe, I am Vishnu,
the Preserver, at least until Shiva shows up
and teaches the kid about second drafts.

Provenance

The hand that would grab the handle

      gripped the young girl by her ankles.

The arm that brought down the honed head

      held the choking girl aloft.

The hand that gripped the weightless haft

      flattened into a blade, chopped
      down on the girl's back, uncorked
      the marble from her throat.

Those who'd showered the giant with praise
found him wandering vaguely, covered
in the splattered blood, brains and marrow
of his murdered wife and children.

My mother told me she couldn't remember
the day when she had been saved
by a large man who some years on
hefted an axe

      and fathered this poem.

A Parrot Head's Wasted Thoughts

Geourgi, a Bulgarian legend, told me
he writes poetry because he knows
it is necessary. I know a poet
from Oklahoma who carries a flask
of tequila. He says he needs it
because bars often screw with the ratio
of booze and juice in his favorite drink.

I once heard that Rita Hayworth, actress
and pin-up model, inspired the Margarita,
which is served in a glass that some say
is a mutant form of the champagne coup—
a glass that I heard was modeled, molded
really, on the breast of Marie Antoinette.

I had an uncle who said he had to drive
because he was too drunk to walk, and I
am driven to wonder if Rita Hayworth's
breasts were ever rimmed with salt,
or how large the poet's flask would be
if glass blowers and barkeeps had waited
to be inspired by Annette Funicello.

Handset Lust

My words float
kissed by light
and melted
to wood pulp.

Like a virgin bride,
they long for weight
to drive them deep
into linen sheets,

the final release,
that leaves behind
the dark proof
to be read—

this marriage
is well set
and final.

The Heraclitean Urn

Black ink,
a white page.
Reflections
of light
and little else.

Lives freeze-dried,
in and out of time
shared by poet
and reader—
a mating of sorts.

Each kiss can
change a soul.
One moral taken
from Grecian urns
and Keats' tale told
of lovers unfrozen
for a moment,
forever constant
but never consummate.

Heraclitus was right.
The same poem can
never be read twice.

Reviewing *Booklist*

I am spending my work night
behind an ignored reference desk,
spending the college's money
on books that will remain shelved
here for years, unopened, decaying,
becoming one with the falling dust.

For tasks as futile as these, librarians
use special tools. Tonight, I labor
with the latest issue of *Booklist*.

Like an old monk living a forced vow
of silence, pen in hand, I sit conjuring
forth new tomes by copying their title,
author, price, and ISBN onto my color-coded
order cards. My deck grows thick as I bite
on a few biographies—Eva Braun, Gene Tunney
and Calvin Coolidge, not quite three of a kind,
but each book received a rave review. I jot
out a card for *Playboy's Best Interviews*.
Hugh's rag without cartoons or centerfolds
should be a major turnoff, but I'm a gray-haired
cloistered bookman with money to blow.

I toil as I have for years, but tonight I notice
a major flaw in my guide's offering of poetry.
Sadly, there are only a few books, but this snub
is not unexpected. No, it's the editors' ignorance
revealed in the rag's sense of order that roils me.
The idiots have placed poetry between Literature
and History, a full six pages before General Fiction,
as if they believe that poets only chronicle facts,
as if this poem ever happened.

Lesson on *Poetics*

As we walk through doing our daily round,
Reading the meter, making things add up.
—*Poetics*, Howard Nemerov

Nemerov stood in the nearly empty
university lyceum on the stage in front
of a blank screen on which a few nights
before a packed house had watched
The Three Stooges in 3-D.

Rounded by age, he had less teeth
than a blind and hip-locked dog
an uncle of mine once kindly shot.
He read a poem the *New Yorker*
had commissioned for the bicentennial.
It defined Americans as the *rejects,*
retreads and fucking 4-F's of Europe.
He seemed miffed that the rag
wouldn't publish it, missing
the irony that proved him right.

He explained some poems were like riddles
and said he'd give a scholarship to anyone
who could solve the identity of the unnamed star
in the next poem. As he read, I thought
I knew the answer. But rejects must bear
their truths in silence. When no one spoke up,
he shook his head, then revealed the answer.
I learned I was right, the poem honored
the unknown dwarf who had played ET.

Then he read *Poetics*. A poem I love
but that night it stung, for I realized
that even meter readers can add things up,
but only a poet can give wisdom a voice.

Reading Answers

For George Bilgere

My wife and I are listening to the son
of a one-lunged opera singer, the one
time star pupil of Howard Nemerov, read.
The students seated around us, now pleased
with the ease with which they'll earn
their extra credit, begin to unfold and relax.
They lean into his words. When he knows
he has them, he sets the hook and begins to reel
them in by asking if they know which woman
of myth might have taken the bite out
of the logo on the back of his laptop.

Cocksure comparative lit majors reply,
Eve! While this shy kid behind us whispers,
No, it's Snow White. I look at my wife. We try
to stifle our laughter, while up from the back
of my mind trudges Nemerov's poem *Poetics*
in which he wrote that poetry is the business
in which one mistake can be redeemed by the next.
So now I'm thinking this kid might have a future,
granted not one with a tenure track, but in weaving
the threads of unrelated tales into poems.

Because look, I know my wife and I
wouldn't have lasted, and Snow White
would still be under glass, hell, none of us
would even be here, if Eve hadn't been able
to teach Adam just how much could be made
right with the simple act of one good kiss.

The Burden of Genius

Columbo, the unkempt first grader who wears
a slicker rain or shine, is learning that he will
never fit in. Sure there's his eerie glass eye
and those brown patent leather ankle-high boots
that make him stand out, but it's what he notices,
those little inconsistencies in the teacher's
stories that the other kids lap up, that casts
him from the pack. He can't help it if her tales
don't make sense. Take *Cinderella*, the glass
slippers don't turn back. Everything else
does; and when he points out this fact, the teacher
says, *Frankie dear, it's only a story.* Classmates
turn into parrots and sing, *Frankie dear*
all day long, so he keeps to himself the idea
that the slippers might not be an error, but a clue.
The whole thing points to another pair of shoes
given beforehand by the Fairy Godmother
to the Prince, the two working in cahoots to smooth
a beautiful working girl's sudden rise in status.

Columbo and the Three Bears

Mrs. DiFiori sits rereading the story, yet again;
the one that never made sense; it's so obvious
to him that there are serious flaws in the girl's
story, or is it an alibi? An alternate version
begins to form under his mop of black hair.

He can see Goldilocks standing on a chair,
trying to reach the back corner of an open
wall safe. Just as she manages to grab
a pearl necklace, the chair leg,
the only one still on the ground,
snaps. She falls hard but is unharmed.

In the distance, she can hear the Three Bears roaring.
Their bellows are getting closer. *What to do?*
Her cunning mind quickly devises a scheme.
She pockets the necklace, closes the safe,
puts the broken chair back in its spot,
bounces up and down on the two other chairs,
sprints into the kitchen, gobbles down
the smallest bowl of porridge, sticks a spoon
in the other two bowls, bolts upstairs,
throws back the covers on the biggest beds
and pretends to sleep in the smallest. She hears
the bears downstairs. She keeps her eyes closed
and waits to be found—her cue to spin her lies.

Baby Bear finally finds her in his bed.
She's thinking these aren't the brightest
bears in the forest, yet in the presence
of three miffed bears of various sizes, acting
frightened is a cinch. She tells them how
she had gone for a walk and got hopelessly lost,
how she found the cottage and says she tried
the furniture, the porridge and the beds,
how only one ever suited her just right.

She ends the tale with some on-demand tears.
Mama Bear buckles, loses her anger.
She expresses her concern for Goldilocks
and insists on calling the police who will aid
the lost girl in finding her way back home.

Columbo enters the scene, in a blue uniform
with a huge tin star on his chest. He listens
to the girl's story and shocks the Bears
when he asks their guest to empty her pockets.
Mama Bear, who happens to sound exactly like
his still seated and reading teacher
says, *Officer Columbo, this is an outrage!*

Columbo replies, *I'm sorry ma'am, but her story,*
it bothers me. You see, it's all wrong; it doesn't add up.
For one thing I don't think she sampled all three bowls
of porridge. I mean, it's physics. There's just no way
your larger bowl could have cooled quicker than your son's.
And another thing, your son weighs in at what, 150 pounds?
And I'm guessing Goldie here goes maybe 90 pounds tops.
Why would the chair break? So I don't think she ever sat
on it. No, I think she used it to stand on. It's the easiest
to move. When I came in I happened to notice that picture
on that wall over there. It's crooked, and there's sawdust
beneath it. Ma'am, you wouldn't happen to have a wall safe?

Happy Ending

So once the lights went out, the actors
and the weeping Faye Wray left in limos,
and the crew began breaking down the set,
and the grips started rolling up miles of wire,
some poor cop stood there wondering
what the hell he could do with a mountain
of gorilla that was blocking midtown traffic,
when a leather-lunged New Yorker
fresh from a long soup kitchen line,
dressed in his dingy depression-era clothes,
saw the carcass of the fallen King Kong
and yelled, *Monkey meat for everyone!*

The Way it Is

I keep having this dream. I'm sitting
in the balcony of an old movie house,
watching *It's a Wonderful Life* in 3-D
while chewing on salty and stale popcorn
that I can't wash down with a jumbo cup
of warm flat coke. The corn coheres into a gum
that I tongue and begin to blow into bubbles,
large bubbles as big as my head until one
explodes, covers my face in a gummy goo,
blinding my red and blue cardboard glasses,
so I take them off and try to scrape the lenses
clean. In the pale glow of blue light
bouncing off the screen, I look around
and notice everyone else in the crowd
is wearing *Win one for the Gipper* buttons.
On the blurred screen, the film reaches
the part where the kindly Uncle Billy
taunts Mr. Potter (or is that Dick Cheney,
but no matter) and hands him by mistake
the Bailey's Building and Loan deposit
which spells his nephew George's doom,
and the crowd goes crazy and bursts
into a wild applause. I can't wake up.

Taxed

Long ago they mined the gold,
but they didn't fill the potholes
that were left in all of our streets.
If it'll repave 'em, raise my taxes, please.

Under the bridge there ain't no troll
just voodoo economics taking a toll
on the foreclosed-on American family.
If it'll bail 'em out, raise my taxes, please.

Kids taking classes at the university
piling up the bills for tuition and fees.
They won't ever live a life debt-free.
If it'll give 'em aid, raise my taxes, please.

Where the teacher stood there's just a desk
with a bubble reading information kiosk
that'll turn our kids into test taking machines.
If it'll save creativity, raise my taxes, please.

Coming home from a party drunk on tea
some patriot wrapped his car around a tree.
Too bad the town can't pay cops or EMTs.
If it'll save even him, raise my taxes, please.

No insurance, then it's on your knees.
Pray to be saved from preventable disease
or better yet make a home overseas.
If it'll cure us, raise my taxes, please.

Folks, look around and don't fight it.
Remember, we are one people united.
A buck spent on you is a buck spent on me.
Let's help each other out. Raise our taxes, please.

An Old Man Looks at Leadership

If it is the wise man who knows
what he does not know, then what
to make of the cocksure who yells,
Follow me! The Donner Party
had its leader, as did the Lost
Squadron, The Light Brigade
and Pickett's Charge. The Titanic
had its captain. General Custer
and Charlie Manson had pizzazz.

Even the greats had their faults.
Somewhere near the back of the pack
of the footsore wandering Jews
some graybeard was muttering,
*Oy, Moses the putz, like packing
a compass or better yet a map
would have been too much to ask?*

The older I get the wearier
I become of leaders. Give me
a keeper, someone comfortable
in his ignorance who knows
that newer is not always better,
and I will gladly follow him
and lick his hand as it turns
the key that locks my cage.

After the Roll

John Wayne, our foster father, raised
a generation of boys fathered by men
who lived to prove they were cut
from the quiet man's cloth—tight-lipped,
hard-living with a swagger. Like the Duke,
they all went to war and took out brigades
of Krauts and Japs with a few grenades
and starter pistols. They never cried
or bled much. When they got winged,
drop-dead gorgeous nurses patched
them up. They nursed their pain
with liquor and proved to each other
that they were men among men
who never cried or said *I love you.*
They went through life poker faced
except when anger got the best of them
which they expressed with a good,
Why I oughta! followed by a fist or two.
These men kept their secrets, their battles,
their wars to themselves until the final credits
rolled. And we, their sons, are left wondering
just what a best boy is supposed to do.

Clint Hartung Remembers

All I ever wanted to do was make
a living. It was different back then.
We bought our own cleats and gloves.
We even bought the white socks
that went under the hose. Plumbers
bought their own wrenches, so we
didn't think much of it. When I moved
down here to Sinton to play semi-pro
ball and work for Plymouth Oil, I didn't
take a pay cut. Anyway, no one would know
me now if Mueller hadn't of snapped his ankle
sliding into third. I'm not sure why Leo
sent me in to run, but he did, so there
I was taking a lead, and Thompson was up
at bat. He had this hole in his swing;
everyone knew it. He couldn't hit anything
up and in. I mean I might have drilled dry wells
for Plymouth that were smaller, and Branca
threw this good heater up and in, and Bobby
swings, and don't tell me about him having
the signs either, because that's all nonsense.
Anyway, he swings and bingo, all of a sudden
it's blind squirrel and acorn time. The ball
just kept climbing to left, over Pafko, over
the wall, and I was over the moon. I come
down the line skipping and hopping like
some kid in Hondo hearing the circus
is coming to town. National League champs!
And now fifty years later a reporter
for *Sports Illustrated* wants to come down
here and talk to me, and what can I say
except I was just trying to make a living.

Solitude

Michael Collins remained in *Columbia*
as the *Eagle* landed below him, orbiting
into complete radio silence, cut off
from all of mankind as he flew over
the dark side of the moon. Some worried
the isolation might drive him mad,
but he claimed he never felt lonely,
just *truly alone,* which he said felt
like a great self-awareness—a confidence
that bordered on exultation.

My wife has travelled to Berlin again
this summer to visit our daughter.
I'm standing in the Portland HEB
trying to decide between pepperoni
or four cheese pizza, DiGiorno
or Red Baron, when this guy
standing behind me begins to whine
into his iPhone, *Geez honey,*
I don't know; there's just so many
kinds of frozen peas, and geez dear,
I don't want to be wrong again.
He begins to read off the brands
and varieties. I so want to slap
some sense into him, but instead
I throw all four pizzas into my cart
and head off to the conveying blackness
of checkout counter 11, where I begin
to look forward to my meal, eaten in silence.

Prisoners

Chained to the mundane,
they tote their cells.
Walled off from the *here
and now* by thick bars,
they serve the *there
and then,* chained
to technology, sentenced
to something less than life.

Oblivion

A Cadillac Escalade
escaping damnation
at the speed of a bat
pulls in behind me,
blots out the sun,
consumes my rearview.

The woman behind its wheel
wears a grey suit, helmet hair,
and plenty of Mary Kay.
She speaks into a cell phone,
her right hand leaves
the steering wheel so she
can gesticulate madly.

I worry my Civic
will soon become
the infant in a set
of steel nesting dolls.

Two inches off my rear
bumper I hear her brake,
see her grab the wheel
and veer hard to the left.
She cuts off an oncoming rig.
Air brakes, air horn.

She passes my window.
Still talking, she swerves
back into my lane
and decelerates. As I brake,
I learn she has two children,
Lane and Brittany. They wear
numbers nine and fourteen
on their soccer team.

I'm grateful when she
floors it and disappears.

Show Business

Small children in Nuevo Progresso
wear layers of dirt on worn clothes
as they work cheap squeeze boxes
in and out and in.... They half-sing
half-shout old corridos, their bluesy
voices, low and raspy, aged beyond
what the tourists think possible.

Their faces red and drenched
in snot and sweat, they stand
next to their squatting mothers
who keep their heads down
and their hands out.

The Oracle's Art

Aunt Julia loved to snap photographs.
Normally mouse-like, she dominated
family gatherings—demanding cheese
from those she trapped and lined up
to pose against a wall, to be shot
by her solar flash. She executed
her art until our rooms filled
with the glow of floating blue dots.

With her developed film, she traveled
the family circuit to show off her exposures.
When she visited us, we sat in a line
on our long brown couch, knowing
before she opened her drug store envelope
that we were about to see badly skewed
and off-centered photos of shoes, knees,
headless shirts, beer bellies in stretched
sweaters, and the occasional blurred ear lobe.
We tried not to laugh as Julia, sitting
on the sofa's center cushion, told us
in all her seriousness what each photo
really showed—how each of our missed
faces looked, what we thought, how we felt.

One Man's Garbage...

I spent my college summers hanging off the back
of a garbage truck, partnered with an old-timer
who didn't mind the work and loved the perks.

Through the flies and stench, like an ancient seer
pondering the entrails of fallen eagles searching
for omens, my fellow G-man eyed the contents
of each hefted can or plastic bag torn open
by compacting jaws. He spent his days cursing
the inventor of disposable diapers and rescuing
clothes that still had wear. He counted beer
and whiskey empties, noting types and brands.
He read the labels of empty prescription drug
containers, giving each one a shake just in case.
He gave dramatic readings of perfumed love letters,
the best of which he said were always authored
in illicit trysts. He kept an eye out for the magazines
that most married men hid in their bedroom drawers.
He believed that perfection, even the airbrushed kind,
should not be discarded. His collection grew daily.

He told me, *G-men are the anti-Claus; we don't bring
them presents; we just haul their crap away.*
He let slip a grin that hinted at a soiled omniscience
as he kept his list of what everyone valued least.

Library Patrons and Conservation

The wild-haired slightly crazed Jesus
Freak sat each day stinking mightily
behind a public access PC.
After tightening an ancient bicycle helmet,
he cruised the web, googling for God,
the Holy Ghost and other matters of faith.

What he found he printed, mountains
of unbound paper that he squeezed
into plastic grocery bags. Each night
he pedaled off, balancing the extra
weight of his newly acquired knowledge.

One day while armored for action
he embarked on a cyber-quest
seeking visitations of the Virgin,
but other women came to call,
pop-up jezebels promising
to be hot, wet and waiting just
for him. With the first click, Jesus
fell from his name. The Freak
now spends lost days in search
of free flesh or loudly banging
computer keys, combing for sex
in seedy chat rooms until closing.

Staff members have been directed
by our boss to let the Freak chat
since he now consumes much less
paper than prior to his conversion.

I often imagine the trees this command
has saved. In one I see a sated serpent
slackened on a thick limb eying
thankfully the tree's darkly ripened fruit.

The Naked Truth

I knew where those women hid. I found
them that time my mother sent me
to stow her mate's just washed underwear
into his top dresser drawer, and there beneath
his last pair of clean briefs, I caught a glimpse
of a glossy cover. A nearly naked temptress
beckoned to me, *Don't be shy. Turn the page.*

I had no idea what I'd find there, but I would learn
with every chance I got to return. I memorized
their curves, rolls, shadows, and even their names.
I feared the possibility of parental footfalls, so I stood
there dumbly, numb like Adam did that day
he realized that he was naked but so was Eve—
that moment when shame first mated desire.

God's Radio

In Religious Ed a nun once told us that we
should always make the sign of the cross
before and after we prayed. The first gesture
opened God's wavelength, the second closed it off.

I wonder if the sister knew how many nights
I would lie in bed, panicked, wide awake,
unable to remember if I had signaled
Roger and out. Odds or evens—heaven
or hell. I crossed myself without stopping,
hoping to land on evens or at least to interrupt
the feed before my memories of Linda Ursoni's
blouse and her fully developed fifth-grade breasts
bubbled forth from the back of my pubescent mind.

Even as an adult, I find myself playing
the same game, while hoping that someday
I might cross myself one last time and be done
with it, but the deep need to hide always follows—
in the name of the Father, and of the Son....

Skeletons

As a kid I always found it harsh
when my mother claimed that if given
the chance to live her life over,
she'd become a cloistered nun.

My father, an old dog, loved to roll
in life's dirt. One night after I graduated
from high school, my bags packed for college,
he swayed up to me, a fresh Manhattan
sweating and sloshing in his hand. He offered
me slurred advise. *Kid, ya know if I could
do it all over again, I'da been an effing pimp.*

After returning from my semester abroad,
I handed out souvenirs. I gave my mom
water from Lourdes, a rosary blessed
by the Pope and a cheap t-shirt. I brought
my dad brandy from Spain, a Hofbrauhaus
half-liter stein, and second-hand accounts
of his World War II Pig Alley haunts.

My mother enjoyed her gifts, especially
her John Paul II t-shirt. He stood arms raised
and spread, glowing in black and white.
That it was two sizes too large didn't matter
to her. She wore it often and took to saying
again and again, *I can't believe how happy
the Pope looks.* My father, who believed
only to a certain point, finally broke one night
during our family meal. To her constant refrain,
he shot back, *For Christ sake, Stella,
I'd be ecstatic too if I had a tit in each hand.*
My mother looked down. The Pope looked
up, smiling, her breasts resting in his open palms.
She said nothing. I brayed and snorted, laughing
along with my bent and breathless dad.

A few days later, the shirt appeared, hanging neatly in the corner of my closet. I didn't wear it much and never in my mother's presence.

Nearly Gay Pride

Daniel, in tight jeans and even tighter t-shirt
that didn't quite cover his flat six pack,
stood in front of me shaking like the robot
on *Lost in Space,* unable to compute
what I had just said. Finally, he flapped
and flamed, *Look dumb-ass, breeders
can't be operators.* But Ma Bell had left out
that information on my job description,

and so there I was, this bumpkin fresh off the farm
with my degree in Literature from a Catholic
university, as virginal as the Mother of God,
two days into my career in telecommunications
and sending all the wrong signals. Or was I?

After all, I had always been the guy girls
called to their dorm rooms to talk to
about other guys. I pretended to listen
and care while trying not to leer.

This feigned yet honed skilled allowed me to fit
in as I worked for a company that suggested
we all *Reach out and touch someone,* but now I listened
to women talk to me about other women and men
talk to me about other men. One night while out
with the unit drinking and popping Quaaludes
at the Golden Unicorn, my friend Daniel proclaimed
that although I turned out to be okay, I must be some
asexual freak. My union sisters, who had all caught
my eye slip more than once, knew he was wrong,
so in my defense our shop foreman, Cindy Kalmus,
who went by Operator 69 at work, picked up
the small green plastic sword that had skewered
the cherries in her Tom Collins, tapped my shoulders
and dubbed me forever Sure Alan—Honorary Lesbian.

Keys to Insanity

His keys speak to him. They say, *Stay home.*
Bad things happen out there. They know
he won't listen, so they wait for the morning
his alarm forgets to go off; the day he's already
running late for a primo tee time or a meeting
with the boss, and then the keys decide to hide.

They dive deep into couches, slink off tables,
sit hunched on pushed-in chairs, burrow deep
into piles of laundry. They muffle their jangle
in winter jackets with pocketed gloves, lay low
in stacks of mail and newspapers, squat in the corners
of book bags and briefcases. He knows these keys
are clever, so he tries to sneak up on them, crawling
with a flashlight, hoping to catch their glint under beds
and sofas only to find their doltish cousins—lost coins
and ballpoints. As hope slips away, he petitions St. Anthony,
who, still preoccupied with Amelia Earhart and Jimmy Hoffa,
never helps. Bereft, the man simmers to a boil; frothing
he screams and swears; pillows and shoes take flight.
A cyclone forms; his wife, kids, even his dogs run
for cover. As he rages, he knows the keys mock him.

The American Nest

Birds have their songs,
their dances with bright
displays of special feathers.

The young American male
has his dancing display
of LED lights bouncing
up and down in the front
of his high-end audio system
with its subwoofers pounding
a heartbeat altering-beat
that he believes in his DNA
will attract a perfect mate,
hypnotize her into a trance
and draw her mindlessly
back into his room and love.

Amazingly, the breed survives,
albeit suffering from severe
hearing loss. For loneliness
always spawns plan B
and leads him to figure out
what she is looking for
in her mate—an earnest
display of an enormous
earning potential.

Art Appreciation

A pompous ass on a date stands
in front of my preschool daughter
and me. He blocks our view of O'Keefe's
bleached bovine skull. He rambles on,
his pedantry fanned into a peacock's tail.

He hopes to win a mate with this display
of brightness. He calls on his knowledge
of perspective, color, and choice of strokes.
The cool woman in a suit and heels
isn't buying the hard sell from the man
in loafers and tweed. They move on.

Our turn, my daughter pulls me along.
We move up. She smiles and says,
I like it. I say, *Me too.* We move on.

The Limits of Art

From Babel's tower rebuilt in ink,
the poet's forged bird sings.
The reader lured from below
follows the song to where he begins
to know past what he understands.

The page turns. The song wanes.
An airless night falls. Black mates
white to silent blue guitars. Dolphins
swim breathless and deep. The cold
startles the snowman into melting.

In a park walk a young husband and wife.
Thirteen identical blackbirds on the green
graze dumbly like cattle. He carries
the anthology he assigned to students.
The couple talks of numbers. He likes three.
She says she's too old and prefers two.
They talk of names and welcome the night.

Old School

Good Christ, he muttered. Again
this morning, the tricked-out
copper Kia was parked
in his accustomed spot.

As he pulled himself and his stuff
out of his battered Volvo,
the students took no notice.
Barely legal and oversexed,
they kept the AC running,
her seat reclined three-
quarters of the way down, and he
looming over the stiff gear shift
hovering over her rising heat.
Their mouths opened and connected
as they tried to knot their tongues.

The long-tenured English
professor tried not to stare,
so he couldn't quite make out
where the boy's hands rested
or did not. He trudged past
their windshield, office-
bound, toting his briefcase
stuffed with ungraded papers
on Marvell's *To His Coy Mistress.*
His resentment fermented
with each step toward his desk—
a fine and private place.

Bliss

I've reached the age of self-knowledge, so I don't know anything.
                                —Wislawa Szymborska

The papers say Wislawa Szymborska
died in her sleep. How can they know?
Might not have Wislawa Szymborska
died wide awake with her eyes closed?

And how do they know that Wislawa
Szymborska owned her sleep? Did she
possess her dreams or did her dreams
possess her? Did Wislawa Szymborska

dream of her death or did her life flash
before her, reflected back on the screens
of her closed eyes? Wislawa Szymborska
once told an interviewer that she grew

to know that she did not know anything.
The interviewer did not ask Wislawa
Szymborska if knowing that she knew
nothing was not knowing something

after all. Wislawa Szymborska now knows
nothing, which she hinted was everything,
even herself. So perhaps in her Polish bed
Wislawa Szymborska with eyes closed
became the Wislawa Szymborka who
Wislawa Symborska always wanted to know.

And So It Goes

Our daughter has moved
to Berlin. Friends ask
how I feel. They expect
me to be in mourning,

but I feel no different
from when she moved
to Dallas or Chicago.
For anywhere that is not

here must be there,
even if it's way over
there. Life is a process
of separation. Sever

the cord and cut
the apron and all
other strings until
all that was, is not.

My Life Among the Birds

My teenage daughter raises three fingers
and turns her knuckles to me. She covers
her Texas twang with a fake New York accent
and tells me, *Hey, yuz da poet, Mister
Library-man, read between dees lines.*

I took bird watching in college, science credits
for my English degree. The flunk-out course
for biology majors, I took it on a lark
from the great protector of the golden
cheek warbler—a man with no sense
of humor. For lab exams he asked us
to identify eyeless avian corpses stuffed
with cotton. Stumped often, I would write
down *dead bird* and plead for partial credit.

When my sister and I were small, we learned
never to make the same request three times
to our father. *Can we go? Hell, no. Please,
Dad? Go whistle. Aw, come on! Kiss
me.* He'd raise his extended middle finger
to his lips and blow us a mock kiss. As his
kids aged, we began to realize that flipping
the bird to one's children was less than normal,
so we'd invite our friends over and begin
to coax the birdman into his stale and profane
vaudevillian act to watch their shock and delight.

At the Aransas Refuge, the tower stands
forty feet high. Tourists flock up the concrete
ramps to reconnoiter the marsh, hoping
to catch sight of the whooping cranes.
Casual watchers often point out
graceful living semiquavers, bestowing
upon the common Great White Heron
celebrity status. The proud holder

of three credits in Avian Ecology,
I never correct them as they leave happy,
believing that their time has been well spent.

On this trip up north, I recall how my daughter
howled with laughter the first time she saw my
father flip me off. She now prides herself
on what she thinks is an artful imitation
of the old act. I have flown home by myself
to visit my recently stroke-stricken father. I sit
next to my sister waiting to learn the old man's
prognosis. The doctor enters and informs us
that the stroke has left him nearly blind
and has erased his vocabulary except for two words:
fuck and *no*. The doctor is taken aback
by our show of relief, so we explain that we
rarely, if ever, heard our father say anything else.

Crapping Out

When told to quit smoking
or to slow down his drinking,
he'd smirk and slur, *Ah nuts,*
everybody's gotta die of something.

He expected to go like his father,
a Grim Reaper jackpot-winner,
who after finishing his lunch
stood to take his dirty dish
to the kitchen sink. Halfway
to the tap an artery in his brain
burst; he was dead by the time
the chicken bones hit the floor.

But my father had no such luck.
First came the kidney cancer
and then the minor strokes.
At the end, after months in a hospital,
he was semiconscious and incontinent.
We gathered bedside and listened
to his lungs rattle as his heart slowly
wound down like a broken watch
did once on his father's kitchen floor.

Act V

Again, this night, a granite dream
nearly forgotten—her brother,
the drunk of two townships,
and an unincorporated hamlet,
a busy man who never made it
to the cancer ward, insists she
is not dead. He steals her corpse
from the wake. I am told by the priest,
the undertaker, and my father to bring
her back. In an attic crawl space,
I find her, shrunken, turned to plastic,
a child's doll whose eyes rock open
then closed as I carry her back
to the three in charge. The funeral
begun, my crazed uncle, hot beer
for breath, wrestles me graveside.

We fall hard into the blackness.

Leveling

But I've no spade to follow men like them.
    —Digging, Seamus Heaney

Quietly, my father
and I worked,
leveling my mother's
fresh grave. We moved
in slow circles, raking
the broken earth flat.
We shook seeds
from handfuls of hay,
then covered the ground
with the straw that remained.

We didn't speak.
Nearly thirty years old,
I strained to stay
composed. I aped
his movements. I wanted
him to think that I might
yet become a man.

When we finished
filling and emptying
our watering cans,
my father, who cared
little for words, spoke
what I have come
to believe was his
greatest compliment:

Hey, kid,
don't forget
how to do this.

Good Friday

I once saw my grandmother praying
next to her half-turned down
and sagging double bed in her bathrobe
on her ancient knees on a hard wood
floor beneath a humbled deity who bled
oil-based paint from chiseled wounds.

Eyes closed she mumbled a mantra
and thumbed her beads—
fingering memories.

She told me once, *Suffering*
is a given. Hope remains
three days away.

Battle Cry

I've heard it said that life whittles you down
to your core. As my father's systems
quit, he was bed-bound, stuck in a hospital,
then a nursing home. He spent his days
cursing the orderlies and nurses,
telling every one of them that he needed
to go home while letting them all know
where he thought they could go.

When I was a kid, he loved going
to Clinton Comet hockey games
on Friday nights. He'd leave
the sheet metal shop's grime
in puddles next to the bathroom sink,
splash on a healthy dose of Old Spice
and then we were off to the rink.

I don't know what he enjoyed more—
hockey or heckling. Once inside
the Utica War Memorial Auditorium,
my father turned into a creature
with leather lungs and the empathy
of a sociopath. He loved to ride
the officials, *What's wrong ref, your seeing-
eye dog can't skate? Then buy a cane!*

Visiting goalies having a bad night caught
it often, *Have you thought about turning
the net around?* Followed by, *There're fries
at McDonald's spending less time under red lights!*

He especially saved his wrath for players
who got up slowly after a check and milked
the crowd for sympathy. They all heard
the same bellowed taunt, *Aw, did he hurt you
honey?* But after a few beers, somewhere

in period two, he'd start to really loosen up
and let go with his favorite phrase,
free advice he lived by until the end,
Hey, yeah you, if you can't skate, fight!

Signs and Sacraments

Paul's fingertips gripping the door pillar,
stomach on the hood, eyes two moons
setting, growing larger, staring back
through the windshield square at me
buckled into the passenger seat.

Mike driving the floored Ford Maverick
believing if he could drive fast enough
strong g-forces would pin Paul, sticking
him like a squashed bug to the glass.

We had closed Club Schmidt's and staggered
into Luke's Outhouse, an after-hours joint
that had Ernest Tubb and Hank Williams
on the jukebox. Not wanting to sleep a wink
that night, we drowned our *Love Sick Blues*
with beer served in glass pitchers and frozen mugs.

After last call, we swerved off for the 7-Eleven
around the corner from our apartment
for frozen burritos and Big Gulp Cokes,
the end of the weekly ritual.

And then at 3 AM we somehow ended up
with Paul hanging on to a car for his life,
Mike driving blind through the parking lot
next to our complex, speeding for the back
of the neighborhood convenience store

with an odd and determined look stuck
on his face. I sat there strapped in
along for the ride, suddenly worried,
as a Fox Photo booth whizzed by
so close I saw a snapshot of some kid
blowing out the candles on his birthday cake,

and then, *Bam*. We hit something hard
and went airborne. To our amazement
we learned the end of the lot we had sped
through was guarded by a four inch curb
designed to keep shopping carts from rolling
over the top of a concrete wall and taking
the four foot drop into the 7-11 back lot.

That night the curb served well to launch
a speeding car covered and filled with drunken
fools into space. When our front tires hit
the curb, we took off. My head hit the roof.
Paul's eyes flamed out, faded into resignation
as he lost his grip, rolled to his left and out of view.

My view of Paul's face was replaced
by an oncoming brick wall. We landed
short of it and bounced. Mike slammed
both feet on the brake. We stopped inches
from breaking and entering the store.
Convinced we had landed on Paul,
Mike and I bolted from the car in time
to see him stand and sprint off screaming
something not permitted by the commandments.

Mike rubbed his head as he inspected
the unharmed car. I started laughing.
I couldn't stop. I entered through the front door
of the store and bought a couple extra spicy burritos
and two Big Gulps. The clerk asked me if I was okay.
I just nodded and laughed even harder.

Within months Mike and Paul ended up
in different seminaries where they studied
ancient recipes for rites and sacraments.
I went back to school where a couple of professors
cursed me with encouragement and told me to write.

Part II

Awash

As a kid she picked beans,
so on hot late summer days
my mother kept our hose
running with cold well water
drawn deep from the earth.
Lean black men tired and worn
appeared in our yard, slurped
the water down, poured it on
their heads and necks.
She ignored my father's complaints
and stewed over our neighbor-
farmer's sin of omission.

In black and white my father—
detached and entertained—
watched the *Nightly News*
and saw the torrents of water
gushing from the nozzles
of fire hoses, ripping into light
clothes and dark skin. He made
like Bobby Darin and began
to sing, *Splish splash*
I was taking a bath...

My father's mother exercised
her right to vote just once
in her life. She pulled the lever
for George Wallace in '68.
I was the only kid
in my third grade class
who campaigned for Wallace
and LeMay in our straw poll.
I remember giving a speech
about how the governor under-
stood the working man's plight.

Before he died, Wallace begged
for forgiveness for standing
in the schoolhouse door and more.
But what about us whose votes
put him there? Sometimes I reckon
absolution must be like sweet water
trickling from a garden hose. Other times
I fear the thunder of a hundred Niagaras
crashing down on my head,
flaying my sins from this skin.

By Any Name

When her son was born, my grandmother's joy
was short lived. He had come with the help of a midwife
in a dim bedroom in the corner of a rustic farmhouse.
It went well. He was strong. She worried though.

They lived too far from the church. The priest, a missionary,
who spoke English, a little Polish and Latin, of course, came
to the farm on first Fridays. Her son was born three days after
and now he would wait a month to be baptized.

She prayed he would live long enough to be saved
from the fires of hell. She went a little mad. The infant's
cries meant more than a wet diaper or a pang of hunger.
She feared his death and eternal torment. She decided
to wait until his baptism to name him. If he died,
she did not want to know him.

Finding the Spirit

The bishop squeezed Mike's head like a green-
grocer might check a melon for ripeness. I sat
next to my wife. She steeped in the piety
of the rite as I remembered how this would-be
priest had been our best man and the bachelor
party he threw, how the next morning's hangover
caused me to mistake a Pre-Cana class film strip
for a live-action video. I tried to estimate the number
of times we had heard *Last call* shouted
right before some bar's harsh lights made us flinch,
but I lacked both the clarity and calculus.
I recalled my jealousy over him being the first guy
in our sorry college pack to get laid. Now
there he was, prostrate and somehow transformed.

I had my doubts until the reception.
He stood in his new black suit
and clerical collar with a drink in hand
making small talk when my wife sneezed.
Mike replied, *God bless you.* Before I knew
what I had done, my right index finger
found the middle of my forehead
and moved down to my chest
and then on to each shoulder.

Belle de Jour

When the new priest hit the parish
the ladies were impressed. Young
and big enough to play linebacker,
more than his sermons stirred them.

After a few months had passed,
he announced the housekeeper
from his last church in Pennsylvania
would move up to Utica to help him
with the rectory and other tasks.
No one said much when they heard
she was coming. They expected a maid
like TV's Hazel who could cook and dust.
Heads spun in shock when they met
the rich divorcée from Scranton
who favored Catherine Deneuve.

Abelard and Heloise reborn, the couple lived
in separate houses but were never seen
apart. They became the subject of gossip
and speculation, constant speculation.
Do they? Don't they? Does the bishop know?

At a family gathering, talk turned
to this and that and of course them,
when my grandmother, a tough broad
not inclined to give anyone a break
said, *Do they; don't they? I say who knows?*
Why care? If he sins, he goes to confession
like any man; if they don't, shame
on you for throwing stones. All I know
is we need a priest, and he is a good one.
When he stands behind the altar, raises
the bread and the wine, he is perfect.
Enough! And it was, to stop the talk
but not the doubts that lingered for years.

St. Peter's Square 1979

College kids half-drunk on cheap spumanti,
we decided to stand at the barricades
for hours. As the crowd grew behind us
so did our plan. The new Polish Pope
was returning from Mexico and would pass
within earshot. We knew that he was known
to stop and bless or converse with pilgrims
who spoke his native tongue. Since my mother's
parents came from Poland, the group looked to me,
but my vocabulary was bluer than the Pontiff's
eyes. I feared my broken second-hand Polish
was more likely to land me in the bottom
of some secret and dank Vatican dungeon
than it was to gain us a Papal audience.

Plan B, we decided to consult our foreign language
pocket travel guide. Short of receiving the Paraclete's
gift of tongues, phonetics became our only chance.
We leafed through the little Polish it offered, looking
for some phrase that even Americans could pronounce.
Happy with our choice, we practiced in unison
as if we were again pre-communicants chanting
the Baltimore Catechism until we had it right.

That night as the young Pope rode past
a few feet away, we shouted in our best Berlitz,
Where are you going with our baggage?

The passing years bent the Pope
in half and hid him behind a cold
plastic mask, but I still relive that night.
Often in a dream, I see his confused look
snap around to our direction, and I swear
I can hear him answer, *Too far, my son, too far.*

Sniping

For David Stringer

Zen Masters teach, *If you meet*
the Buddha, slay him.

The Vicar came here and stayed
for 17 years. Each day he dug
deeper into the Word, past the law

and into its spirit, into the Spirit
Itself which showed through him,
as he preached in a church
that filled with believers.

They listened well. They would quote
the Vicar's sermons, sought his advice,
his favor, until one day when he left.

The parish wept, but I felt great
relief, and returned home

where I removed the bullets
from my unfired gun.

Reflection

On Athos the Holy Mountain
the Orthodox monks live their faith.

Pilgrims come. They climb to witness
these men, hoping to catch a glimpse
behind the dark glass. They return

to their day-to-day world changed—
awed by miracles, events the monks
seem not to notice. Some suggest

humility keeps the clerics
from exulting in their works

but, perhaps, to be holy means
to see the miraculous in each step,
each breath of every day.

Lost in Translation
After *Mark* 2:23-28

After mass one Sunday a friend of mine
told me, *You know if Jesus had been baptized
in Texas, some dove hunter would have bagged
the Holy Spirit, and we would all have ended up
with little gurneys on our walls.* We laughed,
and I started thinking about my reclusive uncle
the dairy farmer, and Christ come to Stittville....

*His disciples were hungry and began to pluck
the heads of grain and to eat.* A couple of clergy
members happened to be passing by. Upon seeing
what was happening, they stopped to berate Jesus
for allowing his followers to work on the Sabbath.

The old dairy farmer, standing on his porch,
binoculars raised, wondered who the hell
was picking his wheat on his posted land.
He grabbed his shotgun, ran to his truck
and sped down the road. He skidded
to a stop and jumped out with his gun cocked
and pointed. But the preachers and hippies
acted like he wasn't there, so he shot off
a round a few feet above their heads.

The preachers and disciples jumped.
Jesus kept calm and asked the farmer
if something was wrong. The farmer said,
*What's wrong? Don't you see that sign
over there? And what the hell are you doing
eating my crop?* The preachers started telling
the farmer that the law would permit
the gleaning of the field, if it was not the Sabbath.
The farmer made clear he didn't care what day
it was, *Because what is mine is mine,* and they
needed to stop eating his wheat and move

63

off of his land or the next shot would be
head high. Jesus nodded and said, *I forgive
you your trespasses.* The farmer replied,
Look dumb-ass, I ain't the one trespassing.

Temperance

Each year come Ash Wednesday
my father swore off the sauce—
cold turkey for forty days
and forty nights of self-willed
sobriety. Our family's life
slid slowly off its hard edge.

Each night my parents watched
over my bedside Lenten prayers.
Finished, I'd climb into bed
and fall asleep counting
down the days until Jesus
would rise from the tomb
and the bottle would descend
from the unlocked cupboard again.

Child Rearing

Just wait until your father
gets home—an unwelcomed
mantra the boy's mother sung
often after his boyhood
transgressions were judged
too great for the metal end
of the fly swatter that hung
next to the bathroom door.

Banished to his bed, the boy
 just waited for the father's return
and aged long years each hour,
as he waited to hear crushed gravel
groan under the weight of braking tires,
waited for a rusted car door
to fall shut, waited for a garage
door to rumble open, waited
for the report of the father's tin
lunch pail against a screen door,
waited for the first heavy footfall
on the cold linoleum, waited
for the shrill question muted
by a houseful of walls, *Do you*
know what your son did today?

Jeezus Key-riste woman
don't start with me now,
the father's often ignored reply
went unnoticed as she repeated
the boy's trespasses with the zeal
of an Old Testament prophet.

The wait was over; the father
appeared, a bull of a man
dressed in green denim and sweat,
as the boy stared at the right hand

66

of the father, which held the razor strop,
once used by earlier generations
in an older country to hone
precision into a tailor's tools;
now it would serve to sharpen
a wayward boy's moral acumen.

With little enthusiasm
and less eye contact, the father
said, *Let's get this done.*
The boy rolled obediently
onto his stomach and was stung
until all had been paid in full.

On those nights supper was served
and consumed in a forced silence
which the father chased down
with a few extra beers.
Later, as the family stared
at the black and white TV, the balance
seemed to return to their communal lives
as if some sacrifice had made things right.

Reconciliation

*Any true act of forgiveness participates in the
sacrament of Reconciliation.*

—Fr. Efren Nano

As a child I spent my days playing
self-invented games with baseball cards.
I transformed my mother's well-kept den
into a not-to-scale replica of Yankee Stadium.
The house that Berecka built consisted
of reassigned furniture. The afghan
covered sleeper couch became the bleachers
in deep center. The footrest of my dad's recliner
became the screen behind home plate,
the assorted cigar and shoe boxes
that housed my collection were arranged
in a semi-circle and became the outfield wall.
Four Nestea baseball coins—three of plastic
for the bags and one of tin for the dish—
were laid out three feet apart on the green
shag carpet. A brown ceramic ashtray
turned upside down became the mound.

I rolled empty Hershey's Kiss wrappers
into game balls. After nine cards
took the field, I hummed the anthem.
Play ball! I knelt beside the plate,
a hitter gripped in my right hand.
I flicked a pitch with my left thumb.
The batter swung. Some men dribbled
slow rollers that died in the high infield grass,
others ripped frozen ropes into the gaps.
Still others, like Mickey Mantle, possessed
the great power to lift the ball deep, pulling
Ballantine Blasts beyond the Thom McAn box
that stood down the line in shallow right.

As I dragged the Mick around the bases,

he limped his home run trot. As he rounded
third, he tipped his helmet to me. After crossing
the plate, he shook hands with his teammates,
who lined up to welcome him back to their dugout
that sat below the bottom shelf of the coffee table.

My mom never saw the stadium,
its invisible white facade, never thought
our television resembled the monuments
in centerfield. She only saw the mess and grew tired
of working on the grounds crew, straightening
the chewed up field yet again. Like an ump
staring down an irate Ralph Houk, she warned me,
Clean up this junk, or it will all get heaved out.

And most of it did get tossed that day
my best sluggers decided to relax
out on the field between the games
of a regularly scheduled twin bill.

At first, my grief paled and confused her,
but she regrouped to say, *Some lessons
are harder than others. Besides, son,
you were warned, and what's done is done.*

Still, I managed to keep a silent hope
that those cards had not been banned
but only suspended by a commissioner
whose punishments were known to be just.
Surely, she had thought this case through.
Once my lesson had been well learned, the Mick
and the others would return from a secret place
to resume their careers. But as each birthday,
Christmas and Easter passed, I realized my cards,
like Gehrig and Ruth after their numbers
had been retired, were gone for good,
but not forgotten. When we were teens, my sister
bought me the *I'd be rich, but my mother threw out*

my baseball cards t-shirt, and I wore it everywhere.
One semester while in graduate school, I sold
my Roses and Carews to pay for books.
I couldn't resist reporting back that my Mantles
could have covered my tuition and fees as well.

By the time my son was playing Pokemon
games with cards that I failed to understand,
the baseball card market had crashed,
and I realized that belting tin foil balls
for home runs with my cardboard heroes
had done little to preserve their value.

They were worth even less that night as I sat
my watch next to her bed at the cancer hospice.
Sedated she mostly slept, so the sudden sound
of her voice shook me, but not nearly as much
as her words which offered the grace to absolve us
both. *Son, I'm sorry... those damned baseball cards.*

A Father's Confession

Bless me my children for I have sinned
against you. In your infancy,
I often feigned sleep, listened
to your cries until they roused
your mother who would stumble
into her slippers and then stagger
down the hall and into your rooms.

And I have lied to each of you.
Remember when your t-ball coach
yelled to cover third, so you dove
on the base like a GI covering
a hot grenade, how you refused to move
when the kid on the other team tried
to round the corner? That was not a mistake
that everyone makes. Rudolph never ate
the hay you made me place on the roof.
Santa never downed your eggnog.
Bambi's mother was not shot
with a tranquillizing dart and shipped
to a zoo. Goldfish don't sleep belly up,
nor do they vacation in toilet bowls.
I am not sure that fairy godmothers
or guardian angels actually exist.

For my countless outbursts of anger,
for the time you spent fearing my temper,
for the hours I spent ignoring you as I watched
sports, or sat on this worn green couch
filling notebooks with endless drafts
of forgettable poems, for these transgressions
and for all of those that I have left
unsaid, please know that I am heartily sorry.
Know also that I pray the two of you
will thrive, find love, and will someday

learn to forgive your father as I learned
to absolve mine, and he did in kind.

Thinking Out of the Box

After years of sitting on cold folding chairs
and kneeling on the parish hall's linoleum
floors, the small stone chapel had been built.

As the women swept and polished, and the men
of St. George's worked with their own tools
to screw the wooden pews into the stone
floors, my mother noticed an absence.

She began pacing the small church knowing
she had to be wrong, but try as she might
she could not picture where it would fit,
so finally she asked, *So Father Emil,*
where is the confessional going to go?

The proud friar who had designed the church
stopped smiling. His eyes danced
like small game snagged in a trap.
Finally he began to laugh, *Stella,*
I guess I'm just going to have to trust you.

Resonance

The confessional at St George's
sat on the wing of the altar.
Forgotten in the blueprints,
the parish improvised
and placed a screen and kneeler
in what had been planned to be
a second entrance to the altar.

This meant the priest sat in a corner
of the sacristy which meant nothing
to me until I became an altar boy.
Then I learned that the whispered
admissions of sins echoed off
and were amplified by the church's
stone walls. Waves of guilt bounced
to me as I donned my hassock,
filled cruets with wine and water,
lit the taper to ready the candles.

I tried not to listen, and I easily ignored
the whispered pettiness that occupied
the priest's time and our shared air waves.
But when a real sin resounded off the walls,
I found myself slipping out to the altar
to double check the candles and cruets.
I caught a glimpse of the adulterers,
abusers and users and learned the dowdy
could be desired as much as the beautiful,
the rich felt as burdened as the poor,
and anyone could turn on those they loved.

Throwing Hail Marys

Back from the box I knelt
next to my sister who asked,
So watchya get? Embarrassed
I replied, *Six Hail Marys
and two Our Fathers. You got
Our Fathers. Holy cow! You didn't
tell him the truth did you?*

The foundation of the Church
as I knew it shook. *Look,*
she said, *This is whatchya do.
Confess the small stuff, things
that might not even be sins
like you made mom mad,
or you forgot to take out the trash,
if you want you can go up to cursing,
but then when you get to the big
sins, you say this: And for all
the sins I forgot to mention,
I am sorry. It works every time,
and you'll stay in the Hail Mary range.*
I'll be damned, fell from my lips.

The first time I used her loophole,
I thought my heart might burst.
The priest knew me well, and he
might just try to tease the truth
from me, and then tell me that my sins—
lust, wet dreams and masturbation—
were so evil and dark that not even
the blood of Christ could redeem me
and that I would be condemned
to everlasting hell, or worse yet, he might tell
my parents who waited in the line behind me.

When I knelt next to my sister,

she said, *So? Three Hail Marys.*
We were still stifling our giggles
when our befuddled father knelt
beside us and pulled his rosary out.

The Fruit

...blessed blessed blessed is is
is the the the fruit fruit fruit...

Wandering St. Peter's with schoolmates
a week before Easter, I saw the sign
English above a confessional box
and thought, *When in Rome... .*
I stepped in and knelt.

Bless me father for I have sinned.
Go on, a thick Bela Lugosi-like
accent oozed through the screen.

I finished my litany of misdeeds
and awaited absolution.

You said you did sexual things
with a girlfriend. What kind
of things? Kissing. What else?
Petting. What is petting? Touching.
Touching where; touching how?
Clothes on, clothes off?

Father Vlad drilled on
until fully satisfied.

For your penance say 100
Our Fathers and 300
Hail Marys. Good Christ!
I thought, *If I had screwed her,*
he'd have crucified me.

Back in the pews I struggled
to keep track of the prayers
when my friends reappeared.
Hurry it up, will you.

Trying to oblige my pals
I recited the Hail Marys three
at a time. The ploy worked
until my mind wandered:

Hail Hail Hail, the gang's all here...
but they didn't stay long.

A Better Way

This time no dark booth,
no older man or mentor,
this time my best man
sat in a well-lit room
in a comfortable chair
across from mine
wearing his new collar
and purple stole. This time

two friends talking
like so many times before.
This time I forestalled
my litany of pettiness,
my mental loopholes.
This time I said *Mike,*
it's been a year. I could
keep you here an hour
with all the stuff I always do,
but that stuff never worries me.
What I need to confess
is that I always wanted
to believe, but I'm not sure I do.

My friend shook his head
then said, *Alan, you always*
overthink things. Be grateful
for what you have. Wanting
to believe is a good start.

For my penance, I knelt
for fifteen minutes counting
the other blessings in my life.

Mike then locked up the church,
and we went out for lunch.

For My Daughter as She Leaves Home

In my boyhood, I learned two legends—myths
about the Eucharist. In both tales a priest
loses faith, one while he walked to visit
the sick while carrying a host pressed
in the pages of his breviary. The other fell
into despair and doubt as he raised the wafer,
as he stood behind the altar at the moment
of consecration. When each looked again,
they found instead of bread, slivers of meat
centered in small pools of blood. The legends
state that scientists came to test the flesh
and in both cases found it to be human,
most likely extracted from a heart. Faith
returned to the priests. The transformed hosts
survive as relics, the objects of adoration.

I do not know what to think of these tales.
I find it hard to accept the miraculous.
Still, once you have moved on from here,
should you lose faith in your own worth
or in the fact that you are loved, I pray
that this cheap piece of paper on which I
have labored with my simple art might
become a sliver of my own certain heart.

Remembering the Body

I think I might convert, become a modern pagan.
The Baltic Perkonis, god of thunder, blesser
of sacred oaks, stern god of my ancestors,
holds a certain ethnic charm. But, I believe
if I stray, I would stagger into the sodden flock
of Bacchus. I could happily attend even biweekly
celebrations of his ecstatic and orgiastic rites.

Imagine a religion founded in the senses.
What sins could its believers commit?
Father, forgive me for I have remained
chaste and sober for too long. What guilt
could therapists dredge up from the psyches
of humans left alone to enjoy being human?

But when I search my local *Yellow Pages*
for Bacchean Temples, I am confronted
by an absence and forced to reconsider
my more sober faith. I recall how Christ
kept the party at Cana going. How he
commanded others to remember
his body, his blood—the Eucharistic
sacrifice. But what sacrifice could exist
if neither element was not, in some way, joyous?
Once graced with this glimmer of Christ
freed from Gnostic beliefs, I return
to give thanks for the creed
which states that Christ rose
to reign forever, his body restored—
a bright, blood-filled vessel—molded
in the image of the Creator, as are we.

Momma Tried

Riding home from mass
in the back seat next
to my sister, I turned
to her, a pink candy wafer
between my forefinger
and thumb. I said, *The body
of Necco.* She smiled,
offered her tongue.

Slap!

My ear rang—burned.
My face blistered red.
Our mother, the nice one,
was screaming in the bottom
of a well through stars,
*You've gone too far!
The sacred is no joke.*
My sister's jaw dropped.

This Sunday our priest
low balled the number
of communion wafers
only to be confronted
with an overflow crowd.
He quickly began splitting
each Eucharist into ever smaller
shares until we in the back pew
crowd arrived to receive an ort
of Jesus. Back on our kneeler,
I whispered to my wife, *Body of Christ
my ass. I think I got a big toe.*

She laughed. I flinched.

Holy War

Each Lenten Friday of my undergraduate
career, the dining hall of the Catholic college
filled with keepers of the meatless fast
and the aroma of grilled sirloin.

Steak never graced the menu
at any other time during the year,
so as we papists chewed our fish sticks,
we envied the few sated heirs of Luther
who ate among us and concluded
that our chef must be an angry Baptist.

Tired of this religious persecution
come my senior year, I proclaimed
that I had become a secular tran-
substantiater. For a meager donation,
I would stand above any serving
of sizzling bovine, raise my arms
and concentrate until the spirit
felt right. I then pronounced,

*This is the body of fish. Eat it
and be guilt free.* And so we did,
except for some of the sackcloth
and ashes crowd who feared
the Lord and high cholesterol.

Excused Absence

A tornado survivor sat
in the middle of a flattened
town in front of the foundation
of what used to be her church.
She looked through the camera
through the television, through me
and asked, *So where was God?*

I once met a newlywed bride
who trapped me in her living room
with enthusiasm and her thick
wedding scrapbook. She had it all:
invitations, matchbooks, napkins,
candied nuts, even the consecrated
host she had palmed at the mass—
the Son of God trapped in a plastic
sleeve, kept in solitary confinement.

The Downside of Transubstantiation

One Saturday afternoon I sat
watching first communion rehearsal.
My son, the pickiest of eaters,
returned from the altar rail,
his face scrunched in disgust
as he tried to chew and swallow
an unconsecrated host. He knelt
in faux prayer, when suddenly
he turned to me, seated in the pew
behind him; a new-found hope
glistened in his eyes. *Dad,*
will it taste better when it's Jesus?

The Upside of Transubstantiation

At the weekday mass
when only a few of us
show, we are encouraged
by our celebrant to take
more than a sip of the port
that Jesus bled for us.
As the swig of Christ
descends from the roof
of my mouth, I am filled
with the warmth of fermented
grapes and grace.

Why not Consubstantiation

My friend the vicar stared back
perplexed. I had just asked him
if I became an Episcopalian
could I still believe
in transubstantiation.

Berecka, I've been a priest
for twenty years, and this
is a new one. Believe
what you want, but why
could it possibly matter?

Well, David, I can picture
the host as all-flesh,
the wine as all-blood,
but when this half-flesh,
half-bread stuff bounces
around in my head,
all I can picture
is a Jesus on rye sandwich.

The Island Revisited

because you are the cup
that was waiting for the gift of my life
          —Night on the Island, Pablo Neruda

But how were you
to know that the vintage
would be so bitter?
How were you to know
that the dregs
would come so fast?

So now what use
is this fine golden
chalice; what miracle
will save this sacrament?

Why did Christ waste
his time on newlyweds,
when years later all that
remains is the memory
of His sweet intoxicant?

The Sacrament of Marriage
for BJ and Rachael

After the vows are said and the rings
exchanged, know that there will be bad
neighbors who will fill your backyard
with spent beer bottles and disturb
your life with their noise and stereos.

There will be the boring and soul-
numbing jobs that you will stay in
for the health insurance and the assurance
that the bills will be paid and the kids
will have what they need
and some of what they want.

There will be short hot arguments
where things that should never
be said will be shouted and screamed.

There will be the small peeves—
drawers left open, seats left up,
the hot curling iron left
in the way of the toothpaste.

There's always a price
for the quiet moment,
the stolen kiss, the cold nights
spent teaspooned together—
those near miraculous moments
when should you be asked
if you still believed that life
was worth it, you'd answer

without thinking, *I do.*

More than Bread

Here I am at the HEB, stop-gap
grocery shopping for my sick wife.
She handed me this list: *Cheerios,
frosted blueberry Pop-Tarts, chocolate
milk, Diet Coke, frozen pizzas,
four cheese for the kids, another for us,
your choice, and DON'T FORGET
the Tylenol.* I read it one more time.
I hear her voice, recorded in this
familiar long hand.
          I remember her
letters, when we were newly married
but living a country apart, split
between my new job and her old
contract. Her clothes moved in
a few weeks before she arrived.
I unpacked her garments, found
her scent, her shape. An easy task
yet I needed to pace myself. I ached.
Her closet filled.
          Some young mother
takes her eyes off stun, sets them to kill.
Excuse me, she says. I stand bellied
against a chest-high shelf, cereal boxes
pushed aside. My wife's list flipped.
My Foray precision point pen uncapped,
I scrawl on this blank side
          and try to grasp
how these words—simple symbols—might someday
come to you, a reader I do not know. What they
might grow to mean.
          I jot my notes
about these miracles found without coupons
on aisle five, but I need to let this woman
get to her kid's favorite breakfast.
Besides, I'm wise enough to know
that I must find what I cannot forget.

Silver Anniversary Flight
for Alice

Buckled into this night's last flight
from Corpus, we buck arctic air
pushing south. Light from scattered
towns rises, filling opaque clouds.
White wisps recall drifting snow
writhing across iced macadam.

The moon rises—space heater-
orange glows on false horizon.

The front passed, the ascendant moon
looks through a veil of trailing clouds.

The night air calms, clears, reveals
stars mirrored below. The Metroplex

nears. The final descent begins.

Winter Wedding

The Texas winter brings brown,
dead trees, bored leaves, sterile
rain, and mud. It grows and tails
anything dead that moves,
and when it can it swallows.

It followed the guests in their grays
and reds. It followed the groom in his panic.
It followed the priest, quietly. Mud can
be reverent. It followed the bride. It inched
up and stained her gown. It climbed
her father and ruined his shine. It carried
its reminder: *Dust thou art, until you add water.*

Women cried, especially the mothers.
No one noticed the mud or tried not to,
but when they got home or to their rented
rooms, the mud climbed up onto their hands,
and hid beneath their fingernails.

That night the lost cause was joined.
The mud slipped up to and smudged
the unmade sheets. The marriage was final.

The mud still oozes onto the walks, sits
on steps and stairs, hides in closets
and on us all, waiting for the next feast,
its next chance to swallow.

The Body

Lord, I am not worthy
to receive you, but
only say the word,
and I shall be healed.

With this prayer,
it becomes serious,
hope wrapped in fear—
a sensed heaviness.

Gravity doubles
on leaden knees.
They adhere
to the worn kneeler.

I struggle to rise,
The Act of Contrition
a mumbled mantra
fills my mind.

I join a halting
altar-bound march
until at last
confronted
by the offered
body of Christ.
 Amen.

Surprisingly light,
palmed then tongued,
it clings to the roof
of my mouth. *Oh, Lord.*
Returned, I plunge
to unsteady knees

and begin to drift.

Although no mystic,
as the host melts
I hear my mother's
silenced voice, feel
her light touch, smell
my grandmother's sour
breath, see my great-
great-grandchildren
at play beneath
the pew, as all
gather from in
and out of time,
graced and blessed
by the shared peace
of this one true
communion.

Meditation on an Orthodox Liturgical Prayer

The Lamb of God is broken

broken by a kiss
broken for silver
broken by thorns
broken by the lash
broken by denials
broken on the Cross

and distributed;

given to offered tongues
given at the altar rail
given in death beds
given to sinners
given to saints

broken but not divided.

still united despite the translations
still united despite the inquisitions
still united despite the nailed theses
still united despite the creeds

He is forever eaten

eaten by our doubts
eaten by our fears
eaten by our sins

yet is never consumed,

unconsumed as the burning bush
unconsumed as the last loaf and fish

but He sanctifies

sates those who hunger

those who partake of Him.

Easter Vigil

One last, *The body of Christ;* one last
Amen from an offered tongue. The altar
rail finally empty, the old friar turned,
centered himself to the opened tabernacle.
He began to genuflect and died
before his knee hit the stone floor.

His body landed hard. The gold ciborium
crashed, bounced from his dead grip,
freeing the remaining hosts. Most landed
in a heap, except for one which almost
by miracle remained on edge, the body of Christ
transformed into acrobat. It cartwheeled
in a wide arc until it came to rest
against the fallen Easter vestments.

The stunned parish let out a communal gasp,
and knelt while waiting for their priest to stand
as the hard truth seeped in. Three nurses left
their pews, rushed past the confused altar boy,
began to give mouth to mouth, while an usher
ran to the rectory to use the phone. The faithful
pulled rosaries from worn pockets and purses.
The hushed cadence of the Creed *I believe in God...,*
and the prayers that followed mixed with stifled sobs.

Medics arrived and attempted to pummel
the priest back to life. They gurnied him out
into the cold night. *As it was in the beginning,*
is now and ever shall be, world without end.
Amen. The rosary done, the people filtered out.

An old trustee remained to secure the church
and found the small mound of hosts and the one
that had strayed a few feet away.

He had never touched the Eucharist
with anything but his tongue. Unsure
of what he was allowed to do, he righted
the dented chalice and covered the strewn Christ
with small pieces of linen he took from the altar.

From the front pew the worn trustee kept
a constant vigil over the shrouded hosts
as he felt each of his eighty years.
At dawn a substitute priest arrived
to ready the church for mass and to tell
the Easter crowd the news. Surprised
by the trustee's presence and diligence,
the priest took extra care as he returned
the wafers to the scarred ciborium. He cleansed
the white remains from the stone floor
with holy water and dried the small pools
with the night linens of Christ. He lifted
the Eucharist back up into the tabernacle
and locked its door. Satisfied that he had done
what he could do, the trustee took his leave.

Staggered by events and the lack of sleep,
the old man steadied himself on each pew
as he made his way to the rear of the church.
The morning's ushers arrived with the word
that their priest had never been revived.
The trustee crossed himself with the holy water
that had been blessed by the deceased priest.

He exited into the cold air of the morning
which felt good and helped clear his mind.
He began his walk, a few blocks back to his home
He was sore, hungry and bone tired but warmed
in the growing light of the Easter sun.

Commuting

How far can a fog lift
before it becomes a cloud?

Whatever it was, it hung
above the causeway,
a few feet above each car
and truck, as we drove
over the shallow end
of the Gulf, consumed
with the needs
of our daily commute.

I noticed how the gulls
and pelicans disappeared
diving up into the thickness
but thought little of it, until
I rounded the long curve
near the final exit,
and there it hung
like a shroud, completely
obscuring the upper two-thirds
of the Harbor Bridge.

While being pulled along
by the constant traffic,
I watched the countless
sets of tail lights
ascending into obscurity,
taking on faith that beyond
it still lies the bridge
into the city of Corpus Christi.

Meaning

It's only the second time in history we've had snow
on Christmas and it's the most in a 24-hour period.
The last time was in 1918.
> —Larry Maifeld, National Weather Service,
> *Corpus Christi Caller Times*, 12/26/2004.

Christmas Eve mass—
my kids serving,
my wife reading.
Barely Catholic,
I sit alone next
to the side exit,
on my mark, waiting
for the final blessing.

Amen. I race.
First to the door,
a half-step out.
Snow. Snow
falling, dancing,
reflecting lights,
filling the night,
coating cars, palm
trees, everything.

It's snowing,
I let slip.
The guy two steps
back laughs.
I hold the door,
then walk on.
He says,
It's snowing.
The guy behind
him laughs. . . .

One by one,

the church empties
out into belief.

I stand grinning.
Joined by my family,
giddy, we watch
as miracle
upon miracle
silently piles up.

Book Club Discussion Questions

1. Explain the meaning of the book's title and cite examples to clarify your explanation.

2. The mother and father appear often. Discuss their differences in temperament throughout the book but especially as each neared death. Which of these parents do you prefer?

3. What meanings does the title "Skeletons" add to the poem (p. 32)?

4. In "The Sacrament of Marriage" (p. 89) does the poet present marriage as good or bad? Do the final nine lines make a good case for the conclusion in the last line?

5. Find two poems that contain something you consider humorous and explain what in each you find humorous.

6. In "What I Now Know" (p. 1), what does the poet now know?

7. In "Born Again: Polish in South Texas" (p. 3), why does the poet keep his thoughts to himself?

8. The poet presents both Aunt Julia (p. 27) and the old-timer on the back of the garbage truck (p. 28) as seers. Compare the arts of Aunt Julia and the old-timer.

9. Cell phones appear in at least three poems. What does the poet think of them? Do you think he is right?

10. Speculate on why the poet separated the book into two parts. How do the parts differ?

Printed in the USA
CPSIA information can be obtained
at www.ICGtesting.com
LVHW051541061023
760130LV00008B/671